MW01705780

ESCAPE!

HOW A YOUNG AMERICAN AND A FAMOUS SOVIET SCIENTIST DECEIVED THE KGB AND DEFECTED TOGETHER TO AMERICA

Robert M. Hoffman

Arbor Books, Inc.

Published by Arbor Books, Inc.

For further information, please contact:
Charlene M. Cooper
all@anticancer.com
www.anticancer.com

Printed in the United States of America

ESCAPE!
Robert M. Hoffman
1. Title 2. Author 3. Memoir

Library of Congress Control Number: 2007937986

ISBN-10: 0-9794118-9-0
ISBN-13: 978-0-9794118-9-2

DEDICATION

To my late mother and father, Bertha and Joe Hoffman, who lovingly raised me and who taught me right from wrong.

To Professor Sheldon Penman, who teaches me, guides me, advises me, supports my hopes, and who gives me strength and new capabilities.

To Professor A. R. Moossa, who gave me a chance when others would not, and whose belief in me helped me believe in myself.

To Dr. Margaret Foti, whose great leadership of the American Association of Cancer Research (AACR) inspires me and whose support propels me.

To Professor Osahiko Abe, who believed in me and introduced me to the new world of Japanese medicine and science.

To my great friends from Russia:

Professor Lev Bergelson, who introduced me to the real Russia and who made Moscow a home for me.

Dr. Leonid Margolis, whose unfailing hospitality, loyal friendship, and eternal kindness warm my heart.

Professor Georgii Georgiev, whose hospitality and guidance are unforgettable and whose forgiveness is treasured.

With special thanks to Dean Daniel Tosteson and Professor Elkan Blout of Harvard, who made my stay in the Soviet Union possible.

TABLE OF CONTENTS

PROLOGUE

This story takes place in another time and literally in another world, the Soviet Union of the 1970s. It is hard to imagine such a place and time if you have never visited it. The Russia of today has very little resemblance to the Soviet Union of 30 years ago. At that time, the KGB controlled everyone to a certain extent and some to a great extent. People lived in fear of crossing many lines. They had to be careful of what they said except possibly in their kitchen to very close friends. International travel was closed except to a very few members of the elite. International telephone, television, radio, and newspapers were essentially unavailable. Even shortwave radio was jammed and could only be listened to out in the countryside, such as to the Voice of America. The outside world was almost closed off. The Iron Curtain, although not a totally accurate analogy, had many true aspects.

Food, medicine and almost all material goods except vodka were in short supply, although very few appeared to be hungry. People spent many hours of the day waiting in long, snaking lines to buy whatever little food was available in the stores. Corruption was endemic everywhere and necessary to obtain the basics of life. The Communist elite lived a totally different life with privileges and material wealth that were unimaginable to the common people.

Under these conditions, doing science was almost a heroic endeavor. There were almost no supplies, poor and broken-down equipment, poor facilities, difficult access to scientific literature, and almost no chance to meet international colleagues. Despite all of these disadvantages, there were groups of scientists in Moscow that could compete with the best in the world. I was fortunate to work in a number of these laboratories during my seven-month period in Moscow in 1976-77 as a member of the Exchange Program sponsored by the National Academies of Sciences of the US and the Soviet Union. The brightest young star of the Moscow scientific community was a young man named Alex Varshavsky. Alex had dreamed for many years to escape the prison that was the Soviet Union in order to realize his true potential. My stay in Moscow enabled me to meet Alex, gain his trust, become his good friend, understand his dream, and help him escape the Soviet Union. Alex's deception of the KGB set the stage for the escape. This book describes a 10-month period in 1976-1977, leading to Alex's defection on August 29, 1977, which I engineered and carried out, an event filled with intrigue, fear, danger, and great excitement. The details of this story have been kept secret for 30 years. They are told here.

CHAPTER 1

Becoming Aware of the World

I was a typical student of the 1960s. I had grown up in Buffalo, New York, and attended the University of Buffalo to study biology. I was an only child and lived with my parents, both of whom were linguists. In contrast, I loved science since I was four. I lived in a very isolated world. I thought Buffalo was the center of the universe. My high school, Amherst Central, was all white. I had only met a few students from other countries such as one who came from Germany and another from Hungary after the Hungarian revolution in 1956. I just thought of Europe as the "old country." China was on the other side of the earth, and Japan was the country we beat in World War II.

At the University of Buffalo, I began to meet people of different races, countries and to learn from them. At the University, I had two wonderful professors, who took me under their wing. Phil Miles, a Professor of Biology, stimulated my love for biology. Milt Plesur, a Professor of History, was also a Dean. He came to like me and became my mentor. Dr. Plesur offered me a chance to work summers as a "Student Aide" to guide incoming students. I learned much about life from Dr. Plesur, who was the most popular teacher at the University. The cross-country and track coach, Emery Fisher, was so kind and patient with me. He let me stay on the cross-country and track teams as a plodder. However, by my senior year, I could contribute to the team. Running taught me to always try and never, ever give up. My intense participation and interest in running sports broadened my outlook somewhat, since most of the best runners were from countries outside of the United States, many from Africa and Eastern Europe. I started to have an interest in these countries. After graduating from the University of Buffalo, I spent one year at the University of Rochester as a graduate student and met people from India and other countries.

I began my graduate studies in biology at Harvard University in 1966 at the age of 22. It was a thrill to be in Cambridge, Massachusetts, and to be a part of the historic Harvard campus. Every building on the campus seemed to have a great history attached to it. In my first semester, I had as teachers two Nobel Laureates, James D. Watson, who was awarded the Prize for his role in elucidating the structure of DNA and Konrad Bloch for his role in deciphering how cholesterol is made by the body. Every lecture was a treasure, whose notes were to be kept forever.

My advisor was a man named John R. Raper, who insisted on everyone calling him "Red." Red was a very warm man, who with his wife, Carlene (Cardy) treated all members of his research group as family, often inviting them to their home in Lexington (as in Lexington and Concord) and for walks around Walden Pond. I began my studies on Red's favorite topic—the genetics of a mushroom called *Schizophyllum commune*, a wood-rotting fungus that had a fascinating genetic incompatibility system, which it used to distinguish its mating partners. It was a great thrill to run the Boston Marathon in 1967, finishing 187th with a time of 3 hours and 5 minutes.

Red's research group had a number of interesting characters from different segments of the political spectrum. On the left was a fellow graduate student, John Perkins, a brilliant and soft-spoken man, who would later take very strong views against the VietNam war. Paul Gladstone, another student, was a bit more moderate. Judy Stamberg was the "Jewish mother" among the graduate students. Yigal Koltin was the tough but kind and perpetually worried Israeli, especially after the 1967 war. Red was a lifelong Democrat from North Carolina, who despised Republicans but was quite conservative. As the year went on and the war progressed, people's views seemed to become more hardened. I was carefully reading the New York Times every day, becoming more and more disturbed by the escalation of the war and what I perceived as its wrong-headed goals. John Perkins became more and more outspoken against the war with Red becoming more and more agitated with John often asking him "Are you getting up on the soapbox again?" This period of my life influenced me very much, and it was the first time I became politically aware.

I started to voraciously read and became very interested in the Soviet Union and Communist China and their history. I became more and more upset with the VietNam war and began to think that the capitalist system had inherent defects that propelled the US into such wars. I began to think that maybe the system in the Soviet Union and Communist China had advantages over our system.

I wanted to go out and see the world, having never been to another foreign country other than Canada, which is right next to where I grew up in Buffalo, and one brief visit to Tijuana, Mexico. However, my studies in graduate school at Harvard overwhelmed me and it was not possible to travel.

In 1967, a new member joined Red's group, having just

received his Ph.D. from Indiana University under one of Red's former students, Stanley Dick. The new person was Tom Leonard, a man who transformed his life in a way that I have never seen before or since. Tom was brought up as a foster child, being abandoned by his mother and handed off from one foster home to another, being told that he was mentally retarded. By some miracle, Tom, with his innate genius, overcame this incredible barrier, made his way to Clark University outside of Boston and then on to Indiana University, where he completed his Ph.D. Tom was a thoroughly delightful man, who made you laugh almost constantly. He had insights into everybody and everything he said was always laced with incredible humor and delivered in a very thick Boston accent, which I learned to mimic with much delight. Tom and I developed a great friendship during 1967-68. At that time, Tom was offered an Assistant Professorship at the University of Kentucky, which he took. Going to Kentucky was a big culture shock for Tom, and he would frequently come back to Cambridge and we would always have our usual great time together.

The following year, I spent the summer at the University of Kentucky. Although happy to be able to spend a lot of time with Tom, I was very unhappy there. I longed to be back in Cambridge, where the highly politically charged atmosphere became extremely intense. In fact, the leading edge of this political tension led to a group taking over the President's Office of Harvard, riots in the city of Cambridge, and eventually the resignation of the Harvard President, Nathan Pusey. These were heady times like I have never experienced again. My desire to go out and see the world was burning more and more, but my graduate student studies still overwhelmed me, as I had just begun my research and was recovering from my oral preliminary exam, where I couldn't answer any of Professor Watson's questions, which devastated me. Only the kindness of the exam committee including Red and Professor Watson and another kind Professor, Klaus Weber, allowed me to pass. I then began my laboratory research in earnest.

CHAPTER 2

TRAVELS

In the summer of 1969, there was an International Congress of Botany held in Seattle. Red was very kind and took me and Paul Gladstone along. Tom also came. We had a very good time there in the rain forest, seeing Mount Rainier and eating the most delicious salmon. My urge for travel increased more and more. I needed to see the world and understand it especially why the US got in this terrible war in VietNam. Finally, two years later, in 1971, again through the kindness of Red, I was able to make my first trip to Europe to attend another international congress. I was able to visit London, Paris, and even Oslo, Norway, to visit a friend I made while she was at Harvard, Reidun Sirevaag, currently a very prominent Norwegian professor. It opened a new world for me. People looked so different and the cities, at least London and Paris, seemed so exciting and overwhelmed me with their tradition and filled me with curiosity to see more. Tom also went on this trip, which was his first experience in Europe as well.

I finished my Ph.D. requirements by the end of 1970 and graduated the following March. I decided to stay in Red's lab for another two years to continue my Ph.D. work. This was probably not the best thing to do, and I should have moved on to new projects and a new place at that time. I finally moved to another laboratory in March 1973 at the Massachusetts General Hospital to work with John Littlefield in the Genetics Unit. Dr. Littlefield was a very famous scientist, who developed a way to select for hybrid cells, the basis for making monoclonal antibodies, which are now some of the most important diagnostics and medicines. Many people think that Dr. Littlefield should have shared the Nobel Prize for monoclonal antibody development. Dr. Littlefield asked me to work with a young faculty member in the group, a man named Dick Erbe. Dick introduced me to mammalian cell culture and the study of metabolism of a very important vitamin called folic acid. I got very interested in this area, especially how folic acid participates in the biosynthesis of an amino acid called methionine. To this day, I still work on this project, since the metabolism of methionine is altered in cancer. We are still trying to develop a cancer drug that targets this process. My time at Massachusetts General Hospital, six and one-half years, opened my eyes to the world of medicine. I saw extremely dedicated doctors at Massachusetts General Hospital working day and night. It was a very good inspiration for me. I also met many people from around the world who would come to this most famous institution to do research and practice medicine. Massachusetts General Hospital became my home, where I would spend 12-15 hours every day. The hospital also had the biggest cockroaches I ever saw, some the size of small mice.

In 1974, I finally made plans to travel to Eastern Europe. The objective was to attend the meeting of the Federation of European Biochemistry Societies (FEBS) in Budapest. I couldn't imagine what the city could be like. I convinced Tom Leonard to go with me. The Eastern-Europe part of the trip started off in Yugoslavia, a part of which is now Slovenia. In Ljubliana, the capital of Slovenia, the people were so friendly to these two confused Americans traveling across Yugoslavia, going through Zhareb and briefly through Belgrade. Tito's picture was hung everywhere, but the people seemed relatively free.

We finally made our way by train overnight from Belgrade to Budapest. On the train, we met a young Hungarian woman, who said very secretly that the 1956 Hungarian Revolution was good. I was shocked, having believed that the 1956 revolution was a counter-revolution by bad guys. The lady's comment made a strong impression. Budapest didn't look like much as we arrived into the railway station. However, once we got into the city and could see its two sides, Buda and Pest divided by the Danube River, it was striking. Going up the hills on the Buda side and looking down the river at Pest and the beautiful Parliament building and other structures, we realized that this is one of the most beautiful cities in the world.

The FEBS meeting was centered in the classical hotel, the Gellert. In this hotel, I met an attendee of the FEBS meeting who would change my life. At a reception that began the meeting, there was a very intelligent-looking man standing by himself eating something and having a drink, and I went over and introduced myself to him. He told me his name was Lev Bergelson of Moscow. I was thrilled to meet this gentleman and wanted to know much more about him and his life. He told me he was a biochemist working on lipids and that he was a professor and laboratory chief at the Shemyakin Institute of Bioorganic Chemistry in Moscow. We talked more and more, but he seemed a bit reticent that other people might be listening. I asked him if he would like to visit the US. He told me that he had never been to the US and that his situation was very difficult in Moscow because he is Jewish. I had never before believed the stories that I read in the newspapers that the Soviet Union discriminated against Jews. I started to listen to Professor Bergelson carefully. I told him I would write him letters of invitation to visit the US. He told me he would probably still not get permission from the Soviet authorities to travel to the US. I was very moved by this meeting with Professor Bergelson, and I began to think that I must visit Moscow. I told Professor Bergelson that I would visit Moscow as soon as possible. He welcomed this, and we began to exchange letters, only it would take 1-2 months for a letter to arrive in Moscow or be received in Boston.

CHAPTER 3

First Visit to the Soviet Union

In 1975, I convinced Tom Leonard to go with me to the Soviet Union. The visa application process was complex and seemed to take forever. But, one day this visa came, not stamped in my passport but separate, and could, at the end of the visit, be collected and nobody would ever know that the visa holder visited the Soviet Union. Tom and I flew to Moscow from New York, and, when we disembarked from the plane, there were soldiers holding rifles. When we entered the passport control area, the military person checking the passport seemed to do so for hours. He would look at me, then at my picture in my passport, then look at my picture on my visa, and then on some screen, and then repeat this procedure over and over. I could not imagine what they were checking. I guess it was just to keep us waiting and nervous.

After passing through immigration control in what seemed like forever, we got on a bus into the city. The bus was old and broken down, noisy, smoky, and apparently with no shock absorbers. I was amazed in what poor condition it was. There were almost no cars on the road.

However, after arriving in town at the Hotel National where we stayed across from Red Square, we were awed to see the incredible multi-colored, multi-domed Church of Saint Basil sitting in Red Square. This was one of the most spectacular sights I had ever seen. We walked over to the church in Red Square and saw Lenin's tomb, but we didn't go inside. I had an old Polaroid camera and took a few pictures. Many Russians came by to watch this process, having never seen such a camera. The people walking around Red Square seemed very friendly but so different from the people of Western Europe, being much more poorly dressed, and had faces reflecting a very hard life. We saw the famous GUM Department Store, but the quality of materials on sale was so poor, I began to wonder what is really going on in this country.

We found our way to the Institute of Bioorganic Chemistry; however, we could not find Professor Bergelson. We met a scientist, who telephoned Bergelson. His name was Nadik Abdulaev, someone whom I would interact with a lot a year later. Professor Bergelson arrived in a short while. He seemed very happy that he could see me and Tom. He took us shopping, and we went to the Melodia Music Store where he bought us classical records. We did a lot of walking, and he told us that the situation was very bad for the Jews in the Soviet Union and that he was very fearful about the future. Professor Bergelson showed us the great synagogue of Moscow and the empty Israeli embassy building. It was interesting that the Soviets kept the Israeli embassy building empty after they broke relations after the 1967 war. I guess they knew that at some point the Israelis would come back.

Bergelson told us that his father was killed by Stalin in 1952 during a genocide of Jewish cultural figures. His father was a great Yiddish writer, David Bergelson. At that time, Professor Bergelson and his wife were sent to a prison camp in Kazakhstan as a family of an "enemy of the people." Their young daughter was left with grandparents. I was shocked to hear these stories, but I believed them. Professor Bergelson told me that his elder daughter emigrated to Israel two years before, and this made his situation very difficult. He told me that the leader of the Shemyakin Institute of Bioorganic Chemistry, a man called Yuri Ovchinnikov, held enormous power and decided everything and that he did not like Professor Bergelson at all. At the Institute, Professor Bergelson wasn't given sufficient funds for his research team, and he couldn't know if he could even keep his job. Professor Bergelson told us that he needed support from the West and asked me to tell people at Harvard about his situation, which, of course, I agreed to do. Professor Bergelson told us unfortunately he was not allowed to invite foreigners into his home, and we could not meet his wife and younger daughter. This one walk on a Saturday would be our only meeting, which was already observed by Nadik Abdulaev.

I was deeply troubled by all Professor Bergelson had told me, and I realized that the Soviet Union was not at all what I had imagined and that the situation for the Jewish people there was very dangerous. I told Professor Bergelson I wanted to come back and work in his laboratory for a while. I said I wanted to take advantage of his work with liposomes (bubbles of lipid into which almost anything could be incorporated as a cargo for delivery to cells which were readily penetrated by the liposomes). I wanted to make the first DNA liposomes as a way for delivering genes for therapy, a new field becoming known as gene therapy. He was very happy to hear my idea and encouraged me to try to come back to work with him.

After that meeting with Professor Bergelson, Tom and I visited St. Petersburg (then called Leningrad), having gone there by train, and we saw that spectacularly beautiful city. We visited the Hermitage Museum and saw the magnificent but overwhelming art collection. We visited many other wonderful buildings and monuments of this historic city and center of the Bolshevik Revolution of

1917. We also visited the synagogue, where someone had just thrown a brick through the window.

After St. Petersburg, we left the Soviet Union by train to Finland and visited Helsinki. After visiting Helsinki, we decided to go to Stockholm. We found a ferry boat from Helsinki to Stockholm that took about 12 hours. I was amazed that the passengers were not asked for any documents in order to cross from Helsinki to Stockholm. That boat crossing from Helsinki to Stockholm would be critical for what would happen two years later. After that, we returned back to Boston.

CHAPTER 4

STRUGGLE FOR A VISA

Upon returning to the US, I immediately began to think about how I could spend time in Professor Bergelson's laboratory. I learned that the National Academy of Sciences (NAS) of the United States, the most prestigious organization of scientists in the world, had an exchange program with the Soviet Academy of Sciences, the most prestigious organization of scientists in the Soviet Union. Each academy would on occasion elect foreign members. It was very prestigious for an American to be elected to the Soviet Academy and extremely prestigious for a Soviet scientist to be elected to the US Academy. This later aspect would also play a role in my ability to get a visa. I applied to the US National Academy for the exchange program, and I was successful. Perhaps not many people were applying. Around the beginning of 1976, I began applying for a visa to enter the Soviet Union. However, I never got any response.

Later that year, there was a joint American/Soviet scientific congress featuring cell membranes and related topics, very similar to Professor Bergelson's work. This type of meeting was a product of the period of "détente" between the US and the Soviet Union that also included joint USA-USSR space travel. This congress was to be held in Chicago. One of the organizers was the Dean of the University of Chicago Medical School, Dr. Daniel Tosteson, who would soon become Dean of Harvard Medical School. Another organizer was Dr. Elkan Blout, a very famous Harvard professor, a Foreign Member of the Soviet Academy of Sciences, and a powerful member of the US National Academy. The Soviet organizer was Yuri Ovchinnikov, a man of enormous power in the Soviet Union and the one who would determine my fate on whether I could go to Moscow. Ovchinnikov's big desire was to be elected a Foreign Member of the US National Academy of Sciences. Professor Bergelson told me that Dan Tosteson knew him and asked me to contact Dr. Tosteson to try to influence Ovchinnikov to put Bergelson on the attendee list. Dean Tosteson was very friendly and insisted that we get on a first-name basis and said that he would be very happy to invite Bergelson and also invited me to attend the meeting in Chicago.

However, although many Soviet scientists were invited including Professor Bergelson, he was not given permission to travel to the US. At the Congress, I befriended many of the Soviet scientists, all of whom could speak English. I went shopping with them in Chicago and at one point got off with them at the wrong subway station in South Chicago. It was a very scary experience for both the Soviet scientists and me, but we safely got back on the next train.

I introduced myself to Ovchinnikov, a very imposing man of approximately two meters in height with very broad shoulders. He had amassed great power in Soviet science and was only 42 years old. I asked him if I could come and work in his Institute in

Professor Bergelson's laboratory (he was head of the Institute where Professor Bergelson worked, called the Shemyakin Institute of Bioorganic Chemistry, now called the Shemyakin-Ovchinnikov Institute of Bioorganic Chemistry). He said, in principle, I could come. I later learned that these words "in principle" were a great way for Soviets to just put off anything they didn't want to do.

The Soviet-American meeting was a great success. The Soviet and American scientists became very friendly. The most interesting character of them all was a Soviet scientist by the name of Yefim Liberman, who would tell the conference that he could prove the existence of God using the principles of physics. I guess the Soviets, who had an absolute atheistic dogma, found that Liberman was such an eccentric that they let him say anything he wanted. Everybody enjoyed Dr. Liberman. Some of the scientists came back and visited Boston, and I went shopping with them in Cambridge at the Harvard Cooperative, the Harvard bookstore that was one of the best stocked anywhere. They wanted just to buy everything, because even the most simple things, like pencils, were not available in Moscow and other cities in the Soviet Union.

After the meeting, I went back to work, and every day would look for my visa in the hospital mailbox. I had applied at the Soviet Embassy in Washington. I would call there on occasion, no easy task as no one seemed to want to pick up the phone. No visa was forthcoming. This went on for months. In fact, one excuse was given that the Institute was being remodeled and they couldn't have me at that time—a lie, I later learned. Finally, I contacted Dean Tosteson and Professor Blout and asked them if they could contact Ovchinnikov himself. They asked Ovchinnikov "Why doesn't Hoffman get his visa?" After Dean Tosteson and Professor Blout made the request to Ovchinnikov, I had my visa the next morning, October 20, 1976. Ovchinnikov wanted Harvard to think highly of him and wanted more than anything support to become a Foreign Member of the US National Academy of Sciences. He, therefore, thought he had no choice than to authorize my visa, even knowing that I would become a troublemaker. He had no idea of how much a troublemaker I would become! I Immediately made my plane reservations and left Boston for Moscow through New York on October 27, 1976, flying on Aeroflot. The plane had to refuel in Gander, Canada, and then again in Shannon, Ireland, before it could make it to Moscow. When we arrived, I saw the pilot leaving the cockpit, a great big Russian lady.

CHAPTER 5

At Home in Moscow

The day I arrived, I was met by my first "guide," a nice man from the Institute by the name of Shevshenko, who took me to where I would stay, called the Academic Hotel in October Square. The Academic Hotel was a very sparse kind of building that housed visiting scientists from abroad and from other places in the Soviet Union. My room would be 906. Every day, I would leave my key at the desk in the lobby and I would learn very quickly how to say 906 in Russian. Of course, the room was bugged by the KGB. Each floor had a "day lady," who would sit at a desk near the elevator for 24-hour shifts, ostensibly to help you with your needs. However, it turned out that the day lady would have other duties, checking who went in and out of the rooms and which rooms would have guests and who may the guest be. The day ladies, I would later learn, had direct links to the KGB and would do their best to give them a good story. One of their roles was to keep lonely visitors "company," a great way to get information for their KGB masters. By my first evening, I was so hungry and there was no food to be had. The low quality of the food was a feature of the whole Soviet Union. I managed to take a taxi back to the National Hotel, where I stayed the year before, to buy a chocolate bar. It was October 28 and was already bitterly cold.

The next day I went to the Institute, and I was so happy to meet Professor Bergelson. In his office with him was a very nice young man with dark hair wearing a gray sweater, about four years younger than me. His name was Leonid "Lyonya" Margolis, who would become a great friend. We met in Professor Bergelson's office and had discussions of what my project would be—my dream being to take advantage of the liposomes (fat bubbles) that Professor Bergelson's lab was famous for and insert DNA in them in order to have a "delivery system" for gene therapy. Professor Bergelson asked Lyonya to work with me. When Professor Bergelson introduced me to the lab, I was shocked how primitive it was. It was old, the equipment was dilapidated; there were none of the modern gadgets that we got so used to using in the laboratory in the US. Everything seemed in short supply. Professor Bergelson introduced me to the members of his laboratory. All of them were very nice (Galia Muzia, Vasia Kulikov, Barbara Petrovna, Lyonya Barsukov, Julian Molotkovsky, Elena Dyatlovitskaya). I was given a small place to work and a few pipettes and other small instruments which I would have to constantly rewash, since their supply was so limited. Supplies were so limited, in fact, that instead of simply ordering lipids to make liposomes from a supply company, we had to purify them from chicken eggs, which came to the laboratory almost every morning.

Professor Bergelson and I began to have frequent walks outside, where he told me that was the only place where we could have frank discussions, since the laboratory and his office (especially his office) were almost certainly bugged and with the KGB listening. Out on

Out on the street, we were free and we could talk about everything. The street talks would become exceedingly important in my relationship with both Professor Bergelson and others. Professor Bergelson began to educate me about the current situation in the Soviet Union and how dire it was for him, as his daughter had emigrated three years before to Israel and made him a marked man for professional and personal discrimination. He told me in great detail that the situation for Jews living in the Soviet Union was very precarious due to the official state anti-Semitism. He told me again that his father was executed in 1952 as a genocide against Jewish culture. The Soviets would not have a total Jewish genocide since Stalin died with this plan, but their discrimination against the Jews continued a centuries-old tradition of Russian (Slavic) anti-Semitism. This pan-slavic anti-Semitism brought my grandparents and millions of other Jews to America in the 1890s. (It should be noted that a great exception to pan-slavic anti-Semitism was the Bulgarians where 95% of the Jews survived the Nazi invasion, compared to just 5% in neighboring Greece).

Professor Bergelson's laboratory was on the third floor. On the first floor was the laboratory of the Institute Director, Yuri Ovchinnikov. What a contrast to Professor Bergelson's laboratory!! The Ovchinnikov laboratory was overflowing with the most modern equipment and supplies—all of it built and then bought from the West. I would later learn that Ovchinnikov controlled the entire budget for biological sciences in the Soviet Union and controlled which Soviet scientists would get the privilege of traveling abroad, the most treasured perk of all. The young people in the lab seemed to be preoccupied learning Beatles songs and American pop culture. Science seemed secondary. They all befriended me.

Years later, I would learn that Ovchinnikov used the Institute as a front for his real duties in biological warfare. It was rumored that he was a general in the KGB. Ovchinnikov invited me into his office to welcome me, the biggest office I had ever seen. His great size and the great size of his office were really imposing. There was a red telephone on his desk among may other telephones (multiline phones had not yet reached the Soviet Union), and I later learned that this red phone could directly reach Leonid Brezhnev, the head of the Soviet Communist Party.

Nadik Abdulaev, a member of Ovchinnikov's laboratory, whom I had met the year before at the Institute when Tom Leonard and I visited Professor Bergelson's office, was cheerfully befriending me. He would say "Oh, Robert, let's go to dinner, let's do things together, let's go to the Synagogue." He was most enthusiastic. He would even invite me to his place and cook a meal for me. Such overfriendly behavior to this dangerous foreigner, who was already rumored to be a CIA spy, would later alert me that such people were sent by the KGB. Margolis was much more circumspect but truly wanted to befriend me. On street walks, he told me that it was forbidden to invite a foreigner into one's home without official state permission. So much for Abdulaev's invitation—obviously an invitation from the KGB.

Margolis and I, after sufficient street walking while looking around to be sure no one was following us, would dash up to his apartment building across from a beautiful church, where I would meet his wife Natasha, his mother-in-law Marina, and two small children, Michail (Mike) and Yekaterina (Kate). Often Margolis' mother Leah, a professor of chemical physics, would also visit. The Margolis family was so warm to me and would feed me real meals as opposed to the unchewable chicken, hard bread, and other inedibles that I would get at the Academic Hotel. Natasha would spend hours every day shopping, with the food stores having lines snaking around the street. It was illegal to take a picture of such lines. In the comfort of their home, Margolis would speak very frankly how terrible the Soviet system was and that he, as a non-Party member, struggled along as a Junior Researcher and a Jew making very little money.

In the early part of my visit, during our walks, I would discuss politics with Lyonya. One day, I said North Korea, China, and Cuba have real communism and are better than the Soviet Union. Lyonya got so angry at my utterly stupid remark. He said these countries were much worse than the Soviet Union. He said that in the Soviet Union there were rules what you could not do. Everything else was permitted. In those "pure" communist countries, there were rules what you could do and everything else was not permitted. It was quite a lesson for me, who heard at Harvard from Nobel Prize Winner, George Wald, how wonderful China was (he was invited by Mao) and from super-star molecular biologist, Mark Ptashne, how wonderful Cuba was (he was invited by Fidel). I was starting to learn the real truth.

Soon thereafter, Ovchinnikov invited me and Professor Bergelson to his home, an enormous palatial apartment, where his wife had to guide me to the bathroom, otherwise I would get lost. I had never been to such a home in my life. I am sure Ovchinnikov had a beautiful country home as well. What a contrast to the way the Margolis family lived. So much for equality in the Workers Paradise.

Moscow culture was wonderful. Every night, I went to a ballet or concert or chamber music. In the first two months, I would go out every evening. A favorite spot was the Conservatory, where beautiful music played every night and some decent food was also available. The crowd there was totally different from average. People looked so smart and gentle with many Jewish faces among them.

Russian medicine was quite something else. All winter, there were almost no fruits or vegetables. I normally never get sick, but during 1976-77 I got sick three times. One time, I was sent to a hospital, apparently a military one I should not have even seen. The young soldiers there looked at me as if I were from the far side of the moon. Another time, I got a terrible toothache. I got some pain medicine that got me high as the sky, but the dentist had nothing to fill my teeth with. My tooth was pulled with insufficient novocaine; what an experience! Simple medicine like aspirin was not available either.

Everything was in shortage—pencils, pens, toilet paper, chewing gum, and, of course, most importantly food and medicine. Young women would want to become your girlfriend in return for a foreign lipstick or pair of jeans.

I also spent much time in a big laboratory in Building A at Moscow State University. The University has an incredibly beautiful campus in what was called the Lenin Hills part of Moscow. Its main building was a Stalin-type skyscraper (by Moscow standards). Building A was about 200 meters away. I had taken the rickety Bus 111 to Moscow State at least a few times a week to work with Lyonya Margolis when he was part of the group headed by Israel Gelfand and Yuri Vasielev. This group was a refreshing change from the Institute of Bioorganic Chemistry. Professor Gelfand had managed to insulate this group from most of Soviet life. A large percentage of the group was Jewish and everyone seemed to enjoy doing very creative science even under relatively primitive conditions. Professor Gelfand had a weekly seminar, which was more theater than seminar, with very loud disputes among the attendees. Professor Gelfand was probably the most famous mathematician in the world, but he wanted to do biology as well. It was a great experience to be part of Professor Gelfand's group. Lyonya told me the difficulties he had to enter Moscow State University mathematics department as a student. Since he was Jewish, his exam had trick questions. With Professor Gelfand's help, however, he overcame these obstacles and was admitted.

Drunkenness. Drinking vodka seemed to be the national pastime in Russia. A bottle could not be recapped. People would buy a bottle and signal with their fingers that they wanted one or two people to share it. It was not uncommon to see people lying drunk on the ground. Frequently, I had to step over the vomit that had just recently come out of a drunk, even in the subway, which was arguably the best run and most elegant in the world. At the Institute, a worker in a blue smock would often appear at the end of the day with a little brown bag and empty bottle, which would be filled with lab alcohol by a scientist. I was told that if this desire of the building workers was not fulfilled, electricity would begin to be turned off and the equipment would stop running. Nobody seemed to think that any of this was odd.

Writing and calling home were real tasks. Each letter took at least a month to go either way, I guess to wait in line at the KGB office, which Xeroxed them. Xerox machines were locked away and not available to the public, less they be used to spread "anti-Soviet" propaganda! To call my parents, I had to make a reservation with the operator days ahead. I guess the lead time let the KGB get the recording apparatus lined up.

CHAPTER 6

Meeting Alex

In mid-November, I had begun to acclimate myself to the totally new world of Moscow, going to work by day, going to a different concert or performance every night. At that time, Lyonya Margolis took me to meet Alex Varshavsky. We went from the Institute of Bioorganic Chemistry, where I had my bench in Professor Bergelson's laboratory, to the neighboring institute called the Institute for Molecular Biology (IMB). It was the same kind of building, probably not old but looking very old and coming apart, since it was built very shabbily as all the newer buildings seemed to be in Moscow. We found our way to the laboratory where Alex was working and there he was, wearing a headband with a feather pretending to be an American Indian. It was a delightful experience to meet him. This bright and irreverent young man spoke remarkably good English with an intimate knowledge of cowboys and Indians. We had a good talk and Alex agreed to help me in my project and provide me with DNA to put in my liposomes, a new vector for gene therapy I was trying to develop in Professor Bergelson's laboratory.

Alex invited me to come to the laboratory breakfast every morning. This laboratory was headed by Professor Georgii Georgiev ("Georgii Pavelovich"), a brilliant and kind young man. This laboratory breakfast, which would begin at 10:00 or 11:00, usually more toward 11:00, was set up on a big lab table covered by a table cloth. The laboratory members, more often the ladies, would cook something and bring it to the breakfast and share it with everybody. It was a delightful experience. We would close the door and perhaps 10 of us, sometimes more sometimes less, would begin the day with a lot of talk, a lot of laughs, and lots of fun. The food was delicious and such a break from the terrible stuff at my hotel. The atmosphere at the breakfast, and it seemed the whole Institute called the IMB, was so different from the Institute of Bioorganic Chemistry. Everybody seemed truly friendly, in contrast to some of my "friends" at the other Institute, such as Nadik, who were clearly just on a KGB mission to determine my attitude and get information about my real friends, especially the Jewish ones. I looked forward to breakfast every day at the IMB and to meet my new friends, who also were really interested in science and their work, reminding me of my graduate student days at Harvard 10 years before. I became so attached to this group, I offhandedly and foolishly mentioned to my new friends that I might want to stay permanently. When Professor Georgiev heard about this, he pulled me out in the hall, away from secret microphones, and told me this was a crazy idea.

Alex and I would talk and were getting to know each other more. Alex discussed some of my leftish thinking, which I could see he thought was ridiculous. He couldn't imagine someone from America complaining about anything in their country compared to the country he lived in. However, despite what Alex was saying and what I was learning almost hour by hour, I still didn't have a full realization of the Soviet system and how ignorant my thinking had been.

I was excited to learn Russian as much as possible. It was easier to learn at the hotel, where very few of the staff spoke English, including the "day ladies" on the floor with whom I spent much time to ward off the terrible loneliness of the late evening. It was a great way to learn Russian. The rate of learning was rather high, as I tried to talk to as many people as possible who did not speak English. I even tried to learn to read by learning the Russian alphabet, which was not so different from the Roman alphabet. I then started to try to read the newspaper—Pravda, the Communist Party propaganda sheet. It was very difficult, but I could figure out some of the words and get an idea of some of the stories. One day, there was a story about Israel, with whom the Soviet Union had broken relations after the 6-day war in 1967 and to whom it was very antagonistic. This was a way for the Soviet Union to gain favor of the Arabs and their money and to oppose the "secret" Israeli nuclear-bomb facility in Dimona. It was also a way to inhibit the Soviet Jewish population from contacting Israel. This particular article had a cartoon with a very thin, ugly individual with a great big hook nose and a Jewish star on his jacket. This reminded me of the cartoon characters that the Hitler government would use in their newspapers to incite the Holocaust. I saw the cartoon and started thinking of the predicament of my Jewish friends that I was meeting in Moscow and of the hypocritical Communist system that I was observing first hand. I got absolutely furious. I began to bitterly hate the "commies." I rushed over to Alex's laboratory, burst in, and without thinking just said to Alex straight out, "You live in a fascist country." Luckily for Alex, nobody was in the room and he quickly closed the door and sat me down and said "Of course, I do, but we must be very careful." We then went outside for a walk, and Alex began to tell me about his real life and real dream to escape the Soviet Union.

CHAPTER 7

Fantasizing an Escape

Alex began to tell me his real desire to escape from the Soviet Union. We took many walks when he would tell me how much he wanted to leave but how difficult it was. Meanwhile, I was integrating more and more into Moscow life. We would have our "breakfast" every morning at the laboratory and in the evening we often went to the graduate students dining room with a bunch of students from the laboratory. It was a warm and close group, some of whom are good friends to this day (Eugene Lukanidin, Noona Ambartsumian, Mariam Grigorian, Grisha Enikolopov).

Alex told me that he received an invitation to go to England from Professor Aaron Klug to give a lecture. Klug was a very famous scientist and knew Alex's work. Alex had been able to go to a big international meeting in Kiev in 1975, where he had met Klug and Nobel Prize winner, David Baltimore, among others. David would play a major role, as we will see later. Alex thought his chances of getting permission to go to England were close to zero, but he was hoping and he thought maybe he could escape from there.

Alex introduced me to the head of the Institute, a very famous and distinguished elderly gentleman, Vladimer Engelhardt. Professor Engelhardt was very friendly, and it was a great honor for me to meet him. Engelhardt was obviously a great man. He had a small office filled with books, with no special red telephone, and had a modest demeanor. So different from Ovchinnikov! One day in December, Alex told me that to his enormous surprise, Engelhardt would support Alex's trip to London and said that he would go there along with Alex ! Obviously, this was Alex's only hope that the KGB would give him permission to travel—going along with Engelhardt. Alex had two strikes against him—he was Jewish and was divorced. He had no wife as a hostage to lure him back if he traveled outside the Soviet Union. Engelhardt must have thought extremely highly of Alex to make this enormous effort on Alex's behalf. Not only would Engelhardt have to petition some great power in the KGB to convince that person to give Alex permission to travel, but Engelhardt himself would have to undertake the great stress of foreign travel at his advanced age of over 80.

Alex became hopeful. However, during our many talking walks, Alex said he really would have a terribly hard time with his conscience if he ran away from Engelhardt, who might just have a heart attack and die in London. Alex was really torn by his enormous desire to escape and his great wish not to do any harm to Professor Engelhardt. Finally, in February 1977, Alex and Professor Engelhardt would go to London and Alex would deliver his lecture. To almost everyone's great surprise, Alex returned to Moscow. A lot of Alex's colleagues and friends seemed almost disappointed that Alex didn't take this opportunity to escape to a new life in the West. Alex described his excitement of being in London, and of seeing life on the other side, as a prisoner would say. Alex's return, however, served as a very effective vaccine in that the KGB would come to trust him.

Author (left) and Alex Varshavsky (right).
Outside Institute of Molecular Biology, Moscow, 1977.

Professor Vladimir Engelhardt; approximately 1970.

Professor Georgii Georgiev at 70th birthday; 2003.

Bergelson Laboratory at Shemyakin Institute of Bioorganic Chemistry, 1977.
Professor Bergelson is at right. Author is in last row, center with beard.

Professor Yuri Ovechinnikov, approximately 1974.

Author (left), Lyonya Margolis (center) and Professor Israel M. Gelfand at Moscow State University, 1977.

Alex Varshavsky, 2005.

Author, 2007.

CHAPTER 8

Deceiving the KGB and Planning the Escape

After Alex's recovery from his return to England, we kept having more walks almost every day usually on the great Lenin Boulevard (Leninsky Prospekt). The bitterly cold winter was coming to an end, and, in March, the thaw started noticeably. It was easier to take walks and more pleasurable. We would always buy the same ice cream from a kiosk on Lenin Boulevard for 22 kopeks (one ruble was 100 kopeks). A subway ride was 5 kopeks. A rundown Moscow apartment could be rented for 10 rubles with the proper documents or payoff. The official exchange was $1.40/ruble, but on the black market [the true value], it was over 10 rubles per dollar.

Alex told me that the KGB had contacted him after his return from England. He told me the KGB wanted to know about the new field of genetic engineering developing in the Western countries. The KGB apparently feared this new technology and wanted to have it in the Soviet Union for themselves. In retrospect, perhaps this was to develop their biological warfare program. Alex told me he pretended to be very cooperative with the KGB, who offered him the inducement of more travel to the West. He told me two gentlemen from the KGB established contact with him, one a lieutenant and the other a more junior person. They invited Alex to a downtown hotel room, regaling him with fishing and drinking stories. Alex was the perfect actor and gained their trust. Alex said they were very friendly and wanted to make him one of their comrades which he pretended to readily do. The trust the KGB put in Alex set the table for our escape.

Soon thereafter, Alex got an invitation to speak in Helsinki, Finland, in August at a meeting about chromosomes, Alex's specialty. Alex said to me "How could I escape from there?" The Soviets controlled Finland to a great extent. This control was so extreme that a term was coined, "Finlandization," whereby the Soviet Union would gain control over a neighboring country even though it may have a capitalist system. I then remembered how Tom Leonard and I traveled in the Soviet Union and left through Finland on the ferry boat from Helsinki to Stockholm. I told Alex the incredible feature of this ferry boat, even though it was an international trip, no one was asked for travel documents. Only a ticket was necessary. Everyone would get on the boat and have a drink or 10, gamble, and have a great time. I told Alex we could escape this way. He said "How can we organize it?"

It was already April with May rapidly approaching. I had great pressure to return back to my work at Massachusetts General Hospital. I told Alex the longest time I could possibly stay in Moscow would be June. By that time, I would have to have finished writing the paper on the new DNA liposomes that I was developing in Professor Bergelson's laboratory with Alex's great help.

The excitement was building, thinking about Alex's escape. It was hard to contain it. Alex and I talked more and more. It seemed the possibility of escape may become a reality.

Alex's laboratory and Professor Georgiev's group were always a lot of fun. The breakfasts were wonderful and we even played a big April fool's joke on Professor Georgiev, who had just recently submitted a very important paper to the new but high-impact journal called Cell, published at MIT. One of the young researchers in the laboratory taped up a fake telegram stating that the paper had been rejected and was being returned by sea mail. This young man, Sergei Nedospasov, handed the fake telegram to Professor Georgiev, who completely fell for the trick. His face became so despondent. However, I couldn't completely control myself, and Professor Georgiev could see the sparkle in my eye and the whole laboratory burst out in great laughter. It was a wonderful joke and even fondly remembered 30 years later by those who participated. This relieved a little of the pressure with planning Alex's escape.

By the end of May, we finally made our firm plan. I would go back to Boston and return to Finland on August 28, the day Alex was scheduled to give his lecture in Helsinki. We would meet at the Helsinki railway station, which I remembered well, having traveled there from Leningrad two years previously. We would then get on the ferry boat the next morning and go to Stockholm. This was our plan. Of course, everything depended on Alex's new KGB friends that he would be given permission to travel to Helsinki.

CHAPTER 9

ESCAPE!

I left Moscow on June 13. I decided I would take the train all the way to Helsinki. It was an overnight train ride. I was put in the same sleeping compartment with a beautiful Russian lady, who slept on the lower bed of the bunk bed. I was in the upper bunk. I guess she was KGB too. Crossing the border into Finland was entering a new world; nice looking farm homes, nice cars on the road, people in reasonable clothes, so different than what I had seen for seven months in the Soviet Union.

I decided I would take the same ferry boat again from Helsinki to Stockholm from where I went to Oslo. Again, no one asked for any documents on the ferry boat. I flew back to Boston from

Stockholm. At the airport, I noticed that if you didn't look Scandinavian you were asked for documents in order to board an airplane.

It was a very hard adjustment to come back home. Life was so intense in Moscow. I had made so many new friends. I started to miss my life there. It seemed my old laboratory at Massachusetts General Hospital wasn't the same. New people were there and I had trouble readjusting. I just was waiting for August to execute our plan and taking frequent Russian lessons.

On August 26, I got my tickets to fly to Stockholm. I arrived on August 27. I immediately went to the US Embassy. I told the receptionist I had to see someone to help me engineer the defection of a famous Soviet scientist. They thought I was a crazy person. I was sent to an office, and the officers asked me many questions about myself. I told the story about my recent stay in the Soviet Union and my plan for Alex's defection. I brought certificates of all of my bank deposits, and said I was prepared to give up my life's savings for this mission. I lived very frugally as a student and saved a considerable amount of money. This mission was my reason d'etre. They began to believe me a little bit, and I was taken to the office of two men, whom I guessed were CIA officers.

I told them about Alex and our plan to escape. I asked them to help me. They said "We can't help you, but we won't stop you." I said "Can you give me some suggestions?" They said that the Soviet Union controlled Finland in many ways. They warned me that if Alex was found missing and if the Finnish authorities were tipped by the Soviets that Alex was on the ferry boat, the Finnish police would get in their speedboat, stop the ferry boat, board, pull Alex off, and return him to the Soviet Union. I could also be arrested for abetting this crime. They said the Finns didn't like doing this, but if the Soviets pressured them, they had to act. The CIA men said since the ferry boat ride was about 12 hours. This was time enough for the authorities to figure out that Alex would be on the boat and the police speedboat could be sent to board the ferry and pull us off. They said the fastest way would be to take an airplane, but I said I went to the airport and saw that documents were demanded of people who didn't look Scandinavian. I said this idea would not work. Then, they suggested I rent a car and drive over the top of Finland into Sweden. I said I thought that was too risky and would take too long. I also did not know the situation at the Finnish-Swedish border. Alex had no papers to enter Sweden. They then looked at me and said "This is a 'balls-up' operation. You are going to have to find a good way." I said I still think the boat is the only way. They shook my hand and wished me good luck.

I again took the ferry boat to Helsinki (still no documents were required), and, after arrival, immediately went to our appointed meeting place at Helsinki railway station. I was there by 5:00 p.m. I was thinking again and again what the two Embassy CIA men told me that the boat could be boarded by the Finnish police and Alex would be returned back to the Soviets. I thought who knows what would happen to me. I had completely lost my nerve. I did not want to help Alex defect any more. I said to myself I will persuade Alex that it is too dangerous and convince him to go back home to Moscow to his family and his laboratory. I then looked up and saw this lone figure with a small rectangular black case walking in a very resolute manner. It was Alex. I could see from his face and the way he walked that he had absolute determination. There would be no turning back. I knew I could not convince him to return. I was terrified but tried not to show it, but I guess I was trembling. Alex and I embraced. He told me he had already given his lecture and he told me that he had a hotel room by himself without a roommate, since he was an invited speaker, and that no one would know he was missing until the next day. Perhaps we could evade the Finns and Soviets after all! We went and had dinner and in order to kill the evening, we went to a movie and saw "Clockwork Orange."

The next day, we got up early and went to the ferry boat. I bought tickets for both of us. I made up some pseudo names for each of us (mine was Del Gaddo [Italian for "the cat"]), and we got on the boat. The man at the entrance just took our tickets, without a glance. I told Alex "Let's go to the lowest level and just sit in some corner where nobody would find us." Nobody was checking us. It seemed so simple. Finally, after a few hours, sitting downstairs became so boring. We got up our nerve, went upstairs, walked around, saw people drinking and gambling, and having a great time. We got something to eat and just waited for the boat's arrival in Stockholm.

When we got off the boat in Stockholm, we saw two huge men on the dock looking at us. We didn't know if they were good guys or bad guys. We just sprinted for a taxi. I said to the driver "Take us immediately to the American Embassy" and we soon arrived at the Embassy. I asked for the two CIA gentlemen who had given me the advice and presented them with Alex. They asked Alex many, many questions, trying to determine if he was the real thing. I guess they were satisfied that he was. We were then told to go to Frankfurt, since the US had a refugee processing center there at the American Consulate. The Swedes gave Alex a visa to return to Sweden, just in case.

We were off to Frankfurt the next day. I later learned that when the Soviets finally found Alex missing, they contacted the Swedes, who told the Soviets that Alex went to London to Aaron Klug's lab. Bless the Swedes; they gave us a few more days with the Soviets off our trail. After arriving in Frankfurt, we went right to the American Consulate and asked for help. The staff person said we only process refugees from VietNam here! How could it be??? We escaped the Soviet Union and were now blocked by an American bureaucrat, whose Consulate only processed Vietnamese refugees!! What to do?

It was Friday, and the following Monday was Labor Day. I remembered that Alex told me he had met David Baltimore in Kiev two years before at a big international meeting. Professor Baltimore was a very famous scientist from MIT, who had just won the Nobel Prize and was an advisor to President Carter. I had met Dr. Baltimore a few times during my many years in the Harvard-MIT science scene. Perhaps David would remember Alex. I found a telephone, called Information for the Boston area and got David's home phone number in Cambridge. By luck, he answered the telephone. I identified myself and said I am in Frankfurt, Germany, and I have Alex Varshavsky with me. He said "What is Alex doing there?" David remembered Alex! I said he just defected. I thought David was going to drop the telephone. I said we escaped from Finland, ended up at the American Consulate in Frankfurt, and were told that only Vietnamese refugees could be helped. David said he would see what he could do.

Alex and I had to spend the weekend walking around Frankfurt. Alex's biggest thrill was eating at Burger King, which we did three times a day. He said he never had such good food. Alex was in heaven in Frankfurt, like a prisoner just getting out and going to the big city. Labor Day passed and on Tuesday, we walked to the Consulate again to see if any progress was made. We were told that Alex would have a visa for the US within two days and a plane ticket as well. David did his thing!

I left for Boston. When the plane was circling to land in Boston, I reflected on what Alex and I just did. I felt it was an incredible thing and that my life now had a significant purpose and meaning. Two days later, Alex arrived in Boston. I took him to my little apartment and the next morning I brought him to our laboratory at Massachusetts General Hospital. Our Laboratory Chief, Dick Erbe, was very warm and wondered how Alex had gotten there. When I left for Stockholm, I had told Dr. Erbe that "I was going to Wisconsin on a canoe trip with Tom Leonard," who was now teaching at the University of Wisconsin. I apologized for the lie and told our story. Dick was really shocked but happy to have Alex and warmly welcomed him and gave him a bench to work.

The next day, I took Alex over to MIT and introduced him to my good friend, Professor Sheldon Penman, and I told Sheldon the story. Sheldon looked at me and said "I don't know anybody who would do this." I was very surprised by Sheldon's comment and said "Sheldon, I thought it was just the natural thing to do." Of course, looking back 30 years, I completely understand what Sheldon thought. Sheldon suggested that MIT may be able to offer Alex a job. Sheldon offered Alex space in his own laboratory and offered Alex a lot of equipment. He was the most generous of everyone.

Soon thereafter, Alex got his position at MIT as an Assistant Professor and immediately started to get his laboratory up and running.

A few days later, a salesman for scientific equipment came through and found Alex and said he was also a salesman in Moscow and that Alex's father told him that Ovchinnikov and 20 KGB officers are flying to Boston to bring Alex back. It seemed like a crazy story, but it was possible. I had just gotten a phone call from my KGB "friend" Nadik Abdulaev from Moscow asking me "What's new?" to which I answered "Not much." One of the "day ladies" at my hotel in Moscow, Tania (my favorite), also called and asked "how I was doing," and I replied "fine" and said that "I missed her." Sheldon said he had a friend who would put Alex and me in a safe house. We stayed there a week or so and nothing happened. It was just the Soviets trying to plant scary rumors. All the Soviets could do was plant a rumor and have two of their lackeys make meek phone calls. Everything quieted down after that, and life began to be at least a little bit normal.

Alex would struggle very hard to make this discontinuous change in his life. He married three times in the States before he could settle down. He lived with me for many months. Even after he got his first apartment, he would ask me to stay over. It was very tough for him. But his enormous drive to succeed in science kept him going, and he went on to make a great discovery in molecular biology, a new genetic code for the cell to control which proteins it keeps and which it destroys ("turns over").

EPILOGUE

Alex had great success at MIT. His fame rose and rose as he made one discovery after another. Eventually, in the early 1990s, he went on to become a professor at Caltech. He won the Lasker Prize, the Wolf Prize, and many, many other prizes. His parents eventually immigrated to the US and Alex would even return to visit Moscow as a famous émigré. Alex now lives outside of Pasadena with his fourth wife, Vera, in a home a movie star would like with three Japanese gardens. Everytime Alex wins a prize, he gives the money to his wife to make a new Japanese garden. Alex invites me every New Year's Eve to a wonderful dinner cooked by Vera, where we reminisce about 1976-77. Alex now practices caloric restriction eating only once every three days, hoping to extend his life span since this process works in mice, flies and worms. He weighs under 120 pounds.

Alex was very disappointed that he did not receive the Chemistry Nobel Prize in 2004, which was given to Avram Hershko, his former student Aaron Ciechanover and his former collaborator Irwin Rose, for their initial mechanistic ("chemical") findings about the ubiquitin system, which controls how a cell discards proteins it no longer needs. The biological contributions by Alex deserved that recognition far more than those of Ciechanover or Rose. On the other hand, the discoveries by Alex, which revealed the first biological functions of the ubiquitin system and its central role in cellular physiology were, fundamentally, biological insights. A Nobel Prize in Physiology or Medicine would be, therefore, an appropriate venue for recognizing Alex's seminal work. Both I and many other colleagues presume that this will happen soon enough.

However successful Alex has been and how successful our escape was, Alex's escape hurt many people. Thirty years later, I would learn from Klaus Scherer, an Emeritus Professor in Paris and long-time friend of Professor Georgiev, what happened at the Institute the day Alex was discovered missing. Klaus was present in the Institute on that day and said that Professor Engelhardt was in tears, and the Institute was in total disarray and swarming with KGB. Professor Engelhardt felt totally betrayed and asked "Why at the end of my life was I so let down?" Professor Engelhardt and Professor Georgiev were afraid the KGB would close down the Institute, a real possibility that would have destroyed the careers and aspirations of hundreds of people. Alex's father was thrown out of the Communist Party, which meant that he would probably lose his job at the Institute. By blaming me, Alex's father finally got reinstated in the Party and kept his job. Neither Professor Englehardt nor Professor Georgiev were Party members. The Institute survived but was definitely scarred. It was through the genius of Georgiev and Englehardt's successor, Andrei Mirzabekov, that the Institute would eventually thrive again. Professor Georgiev never forgave Alex. Professor Engelhardt died sometime later, a broken man.

In 1978, I went to an international biochemistry meeting in Dresden, East Germany. Professor Bergelson and Dr. Margolis were there. Ovchinnikov also attended. Ovchinnikov was so angry when he saw me and asked what I was doing there! I said I wanted to attend the meeting. There was nothing this all-powerful man could do to me! I thoroughly enjoyed Dresden and East Germany and found it much richer than Russia. Some people had private homes, many people had cars. The Meissen factory made world-famous porcelain. Unfortunately, I didn't buy any when I visited this fabulous plant. On the way back through Checkpoint Charley at the Berlin Wall, I put my passport through the bottom of a window covered with metal so no one could see the officer. After waiting for 30 minutes, my passport did not reappear. Obviously, the East Germans had learned about Alex and me. I was with Rich Roberts, my friend from Harvard, who would go on and win the Nobel Prize. Rich was carrying his violin. Finally, I became very flustered and then panicked. I began to beat the metal window with my fist and screamed "Give me my fucking passport!!" It immediately reappeared in the tray! So much for the fearless commies.

In 1980, I went to another meeting in Budapest to meet Professor Bergelson. I didn't even have a visa, which I received after much argument at the Budapest airport. I knew Professor Bergelson was there but had no idea at which hotel. I found an English-speaking taxi driver, and after a few stops at various hotels and the taxi driver tiring of this game, I found Professor Bergelson at his hotel. We spent a treasured time together at the meeting. He later told me he was under intense surveillance by the Hungarian KGB.

From Budapest, I crossed Yugoslavia by train to visit Athens. On the train, the Yugoslav police took my passport. I was the only one on the train who had their passport confiscated. It was returned at the border. They did not want me causing trouble in Yugoslavia. It was clear the Soviet and Yugoslav KGBs were collaborating with probably the Hungarians tipping off the Yugoslavs about me. It was conventional wisdom in the US at that time that the Yugoslavs and Soviets, although both Communist, were enemies. Obviously not true!

Almost everyday, I dreamed about Moscow. I wanted to go back, but of course was terrified. Finally, another FEBS meeting was scheduled, this time in Moscow in 1984. I applied and received a visa! I was scared to go but calculated the Soviets would not try anything on me. The meeting was held in the Hammer Center, an elegant new building named after the American Oilman, Armand Hammer, a great friend of all the Soviet leaders starting from Lenin. Ovchinnikov was the organizer of the FEBS meeting. Even the hated Israelis got visas including émigrés from the Soviet Union, because the FEBS made this a condition of the meeting to be held in Moscow since Israel is a FEBS member. Ovchinnikov could do anything, and everyone got a visa! At the meeting, Ovchinnikov welcomed me warmly and said "Robert, you can come to Moscow anytime." I was then interviewed by a "commentator" from Radio Moscow, who asked me what I thought about international travel for scientists. I spoke into a microphone and said it was essential, since scientists from around the world should collaborate. Of course, the interview was never broadcast. The KGB just wanted to know my current thinking. After the 1984 visit, I went to Moscow at least every 2 years and saw great changes every time. I even slept at the Margolis home when I was supposed to be sleeping at a dormitory at Moscow State University. The "cleaning lady" reported me missing, but, by that time, nobody really cared.

During my seven months in Moscow, I lived almost as a Russian. I had the same mostly bad food and almost non-existent medicine. I got to know many, many Russians as real friends and had intimate conversations in their kitchens, where I could see the wonderful aspects of Russian culture, especially among the intelligencia. The tightness of friendships that I observed in Moscow, I never observed in America. I also became intimately experienced with the KGB and their tactics of providing me with both male and female "friends." The "Jewish Question" loomed large for them. In the beginning, the KGB labeled me a "CIA spy," later a

"CIA-Zionist spy." Their mentalities could not comprehend that I did what I did simply because I wanted to. I learned of the total hypocrisy of communism. I never once met a member of the Communist Party who believed in communism. Ovchinnikov lived as well as any capitalist tycoon in the West.

My experiences gave me new insight into the Soviet Union and its relationship with the US and other countries such as Yugoslavia as well as the real American attitude to "human rights."

It was remarkable how the Yugoslavs confiscated my passport on a train. This demonstrated very tight coordination between the KGBs of the Soviet Union, Hungary (as expected), and Yugoslavia (totally unexpected).

It was also noteworthy to see the almost "we-don't-care" attitude and incompetence in the American Embassy in Sweden. For all of President Carter's "Human Rights" proclamations, I was offered no help to ferret out Alex despite me possibly risking my life. The advice the CIA men gave me in the Embassy to take Alex out through the Airport was totally stupid. Their other plan, that I drive over the top to cross the Finnish-Swedish border, was almost as stupid. They had no idea of the ferry between Helsinki and Stockholm. How many others may have gotten out if we really cared. The attitude at the American Consulate in Frankfurt that "We only process Vietnamese refugees" really showed how hypocritical Carter's human rights program was. At the US National Academy of Sciences, who sponsored my exchange visit, they were thoroughly disgusted with me for helping Alex. It was only the individual Americans like Sheldon Penman and Dick Erbe, who really cared about Alex and what I did. David Baltimore never bothered to meet me, even once. Just after our arrival, he invited Alex to dinner and without me.

Alex's contribution to American and international science was enormous. How different things would have been if Alex remained another 15 years in the Soviet Union before the big prison opened under Yeltsin. He would have continued to be a Junior Researcher, limited by the fact he was a Jew and not a Party member, with just a tiny fraction of the possibilities he found at MIT and Caltech.

I kept this story a secret for 30 years, confiding only in close friends usually after many years when I knew them well. Alex finally went public in 2006 in a book called Candid Science VI, a book of interviews with famous scientists by Istvan Hargittai and Magdolna Hargittai, published by Imperial College Press. Alex's story in the Hargittai's book is basically accurate and riveting. I decided to finally tell my side. I hope the good people who were hurt in this episode can understand and forgive Alex and me.

WHERE ARE THEY NOW?

Professor Raper died unexpectedly in 1974 at 63, my present age.

Tom Leonard returned to Clark University, where he became Chairman of the Botany Department. He will retire from the University this year.

Dick Erbe moved to my hometown, Buffalo, NY, to become Chairman of Medical Genetics at the University of Buffalo.

Lyonya Margolis is a very successful biologist at the US National Institutes of Health. He has become a world famous researcher in AIDS. Unlike Alex, who completely broke his emotional ties to Russia, Lyonya's wife Natasha, and two out of four of

Lyonya's children still live in Moscow. Lyonya never could make this break.

Professor Bergelson lives with his wife, younger daughter, and grandchildren outside of Jerusalem. Professor Bergelson's picture still hangs in the Shemyakin-Ovchinnikov Institute in a special place for war heroes. Professor Bergelson is still active and goes to his office at the Hebrew University at age 89.

Professor Georgiev is now head of the new Institute of Gene Biology in Moscow and continues to be enormously successful. I attended his 70th birthday party in Moscow in 2003, but we did not speak about the events of 1977.

Ovchinnikov died at age 54 in 1988. He already appeared ill at the FEBS meeting in 1984, having lost much weight. The Institute of Bioorganic Chemistry is now called the Shemyakin-Ovchinnikov Institute. The Institute is now in the palatial building that Ovchinnikov built before he died. There is strong evidence that Ovchinnikov was a General in the KGB and was highly involved in the Soviet bio-warfare program. Just before he died, Ovchinnikov wrote me a very warm letter.

I now have a very productive collaboration with a laboratory in the Shemyakin-Ovchinnikov Institute, headed by two brothers, Sergei and Konstantin Lukyanov, two of the world's greatest genetic engineers. They make fluorescent proteins, very important to our current research on small animal imaging for which AntiCancer is the world leader.

Professor Gelfand is still active at age 94 and still does some science at Rutgers University.

David Baltimore, after a long period at MIT, became President of Rockefeller University and then went on to become President of Caltech, where he and Alex are now reunited.

I stayed on at Massachusetts General Hospital until 1979. After Moscow, I could never readjust to our old laboratory at MGH. In 1979, I moved to the University of California, San Diego (UCSD) to join the Faculty of Medicine. I founded AntiCancer, Inc., a biotech company in 1984. I am currently a Professor of Surgery at UCSD and President of AntiCancer, a company with diverse and unique scientific and research interests and 30 employees (www.anticancer.com). Life has been a difficult challenge, it seems almost every day. I retain my intense interest in science, and I especially love the practical application of scientific discovery. However, nothing can match the excitement and satisfaction that peaked on August 29, 1977, the day Alex and I escaped the clutches of the Soviet Union.

ABOUT THE AUTHOR

ROBERT M. HOFFMAN

Robert M. Hoffman was born in 1944 in Greenwich, Connecticut, USA. Hoffman grew up in Buffalo, New York and graduated from the University of Buffalo in 1965. Hoffman completed his Ph.D. in Biology at Harvard University in 1971. His post-doctoral training was at Massachusetts General Hospital, Boston and Institutes of Bioorganic Chemistry and Molecular Biology and Moscow State University, Moscow, Russia. He has been a member of the University of California San Diego School of Medicine faculty since 1979 and is currently Professor of Surgery. Hoffman began his cancer-research career in 1973. Hoffman founded AntiCancer, Inc., a biotechnology company in San Diego, California, in 1984. Hoffman has published approximately 400 scientific papers and is a leading international authority on cancer research.